Busting *the* COLLEGE PLANNING Lies

How Unknown Opportunity Costs Kill the Goose and the Golden Egg

KIM D. H. BUTLER
with E.P. Hagenlocher

**Author of *Busting the Retirement Lies*
and *Busting the Financial Plnning Lies***

Busting the College Planning Lies: How Unknown Opportunity Costs Kill the Goose and the Golden Egg
Copyright © 2023 Kim D. H. Butler and E.P. Hagenlocher

Prosperity Economics Movement
22790 Highway 259 South
Mount Enterprise, TX 75681
www.ProsperityEconomics.org

First Edition
ISBN: 978-1-7375867-3-9 (paperback)
        978-1-7375867-4-6 (ebook)

Produced in the United States of America

Published with the guidance of Social Motion Publishing, which specializes in books that benefit causes and nonprofits. For more information, go to SocialMotionPublishing.com.

Contents

Foreword

I was a career late starter. After graduating from high school in 1979, I decided to spend four years earning a Bachelor of Science degree, two more years earning a Master of Science, two in a training program for a large corporation, and finally two years earning a Master of Business Administration. It wasn't until I was 28, ten years after leaving high school, that I entered the workforce in earnest. My career initiation started with more education, a three-month training program on site that taught me everything I needed to know for my new position as a junior salesperson on a bank's securities trading desk.

Luckily for me and for my parents, the cost of college was a pittance compared to today. My undergraduate university cost less than $1,500 per year, including tuition, room, and board. I could have covered more than half of this cost during my summer lifeguarding job and my parents would have happily covered the rest out of a couple of month's savings. However, we didn't have to pay at all! With President Jimmy Carter's 1978 Middle Income Student Assistance Act, the Federal Government offered us all the money we needed to cover this education, and the next, and the one after that! Because the cost of college was still so low, I paid off my debt in my first year of work after leaving business school.

My gain, of course, has led to great pain for others over time. By giving students easy access to credit, colleges were able to charge more and more each year and families didn't pay attention because the money wasn't coming out of their pockets, not until the debt came due. The student loan program itself, now at over $1.7 trillion with 45 million borrowers and an average of $38,000 owed per borrower, is leaving millions of people so deep in debt that they wonder how they can possibly get out.

But money is only one part of the problem with college. The time spent there is another factor that must be considered very carefully. At age 28, I was nearly double the age of a person coming into the workforce a century ago! Also, with so many years of college life, my work ethic was not what it could have been had I moved directly into the workforce in my teens or early twenties. Certainly, the credibility created by a college degree helped me to get my job. But what of that time I spent getting there? A family delayed, a home purchase as well, a much shorter period between the start and the end of my career and life, all things that are hardly noticeable in one's 20s, but become a factor later, as one's "wealth curve" has had less of a chance to grow. Also, getting real experience in the work force is the best way to know what one truly loves to do. I enjoyed my time on Wall Street but found that what I really wanted was to help people with all things financial in their lives. My work today as a financial strategist and advisor is what I truly love, and thankfully I have many more years ahead to grow my practice and to help others to prepare for their futures. But sometimes I look back on those lost college years of my 20s and wonder "what if?".

To bring it full circle, my wife and I are blessed with four wonderful adult children today ranging in age from 20 to 26. When Justin, our first child, was a senior in high school, we did all the usual tours of a few dozen colleges. Like all our children, Justin was a very good student in high school, so he set his sights high. However, in the end, he got accepted to none of the schools he wanted, which left us in a quandary. What, exactly, does one do if all the colleges a young person wants don't want him? Luckily, an alternative education "gap year" program for recent high school graduates called Uncollege had just been founded the year before. Justin applied to Uncollege and was accepted. This changed the trajectory of his education and, indeed, his life and our family's perspective about secondary education as well.

After finishing Uncollege's entrepreneurship bootcamp program in San Francisco, Justin applied and was accepted for a software engineering position in New York City at the ripe old age of 19. He spent the next three years at this company, blossomed as a programmer, and is now a business founder and owner of a startup fintech company with a fellow Uncollege graduate in Austin, Texas. Brian, our second son, applied to a handful of colleges and was accepted to all. However, the draw of an alternative education was too strong to resist and he, too, enrolled into Uncollege in 2017. Brian remained in San Francisco after his entrepreneurship bootcamp ended and has been working over three years at a startup company which is changing the dynamics of the fuel delivery industry. He is a seasoned salesperson and employee, he knows what he loves and what he's good at, he has nearly four years of work experience, and he is still only 23 years old.

Our two youngest children, now 20 years old, have decided to travel on different paths. Severin, our third son, is in a gap year program with Discover Praxis, a company that has been offering high school and college students an alternative to college for nearly a decade. Our daughter, Mackenna, has decided to go to college, and is now beginning her second year at the University of Connecticut. We wish her well as we do all our children. We are sharing the financial burden with Mackenna, which will total about 10 times what it cost each of our sons for their gap year educations. But it is something she wants, so we will make it work. Life is about education and growth. You can choose college, of course, and most of you will. But understand the economics, the time, and what else might be available to you to achieve your goals. These are some of the lessons you will learn about college, education, money, finance, and life from this wonderful book!

— *Chris Tormey*

●　　●　　●　　●　　●

"The more that you read, the more things you will know, the more that you learn, the more places you'll go."
— Dr. Seuss

My kids were raised on Dr. Seuss. *Oh, the Places You'll Go* was one of their favorites. They liked it because it of the visuals it conjured up in their minds, providing launching pads into imaginary worlds their young minds could readily explore. My wife and I liked the story because it instilled the values of hard work. Perhaps most importantly, the story built upon a solid foundation of education. It was only one of several books we would read to our kids underscoring the importance of education.

Back in the day, education meant formal education—the kind one received by attending classes at a community college or a college or university. Education that would produce a diploma or a "certificate" that everyone knew would lead to a better life and, a better paycheck than was possible without earning that sheepskin. The term "going to college" meant leaving home, living in a dorm or in off-campus housing with roommates who ostensibly had the same goals and objectives as you. We all shared the common American value of getting "through college," then getting on with life. College was THE undisputed right-of-passage for millions of Americans.

We valued the experience where, as Ralph Waldo Emerson said, "The mind, once stretched by a new idea, never returns to its original dimensions."

Guy Kawasaki of Macintosh computer fame wrote in his 2019 book, *Wise Guy*, that his Stanford education in 1972 cost just $2,850, whereas today it's $62,000.

According to the Bureau of Labor Statistics CPI Inflation Calculator, if Stanford tuition had increased at the pace of overall inflation, it would be $17,007 today. That means that Stanford tuition has increased 3.64 times faster than general inflation. The bloated costs of an education are not unique to Stanford.

When people who graduated in the late 1960s visit our alma maters, we hardly recognize them. Specialized buildings of all kinds abound, and university fitness centers compete with the finest private clubs. Many colleges even sport climbing walls and lazy rivers. "Student fees," which are not included in tuition, may cover some of this academic bling. Such amenities attract students and professors, so colleges are forced to compete. And don't be surprised if the athletic department has one or more large buildings all to itself. In 2017 alone, U.S. universities and colleges spent $11.5 billion on construction, an all-time high.

Adding to the cost of college is that more and more students are taking longer to finish. It is not uncommon for students to take five years to complete a baccalaureate rather than four, thereby stretching out the costs and shortening their earning years before retirement.

Administrative staff including fundraisers, financial aid advisers, global recruitment staff, and many others grew by 60 percent between 1993 and 2009. This is 10 times the rate of growth of tenured faculty positions. We also have more in the way of services for things like counseling and academic tutoring. Gyms and other facilities need to be supervised, cleaned, and maintained.

The Chronicle of Higher Education recently estimated that college athletics is a $10 billion marketplace. With very few exceptions, most colleges and universities rely on what the NCAA calls "allocated revenue." This includes direct and indirect support from general funds, student fees, and government appropriations. In other words, most colleges subsidize their athletics programs, sometimes to startling degrees.

Compensation for college presidents has also added to the increased cost of an education. As of 2015, average pay for private-college presidents in the United States surpassed $550,000, with 58 presidents taking home more than $1 million a year. The average salaries for full professors at top public institutions have risen 12 percent in excess of inflation since 2000. While schools might pay $250,000 for a famous professor, top coaches make millions. The top dog (Nick Saban, football coach at Alabama) makes more than $11 million, not counting outside income.

Here's a dirty little secret: a school that charges $50,000 in tuition can offer a huge range of prices to different students. Some students might pay $10,000, others much more." Most don't pay full price, but those that do are one reason tuition goes up so fast. Rich people don't think twice about writing a fat check each year. This includes rich people from other countries and states that pay even more. David Feldman, economics professor at the College of William & Mary, tells us that "A college's sticker price is set by its wealthiest students' ability to pay."

Given these incredibly unsustainable costs, it should not be surprising that yearly student-loan originations grew from $53 billion to $120 billion between 2001 and 2012. Meanwhile, average tuition rose 46 percent in constant dollars during that same time frame. Since students can borrow enough to pay the higher costs, schools are less inclined to keep costs in line.

While American colleges and universities are some of our nation's greatest assets, over the years they have been burdened with unsustainable cost increases. Parents and students should realize that post-secondary education is a business... a very big business. They are there to educate but they are also there to make money. In fact, wise parents and students should recognize that these institutions are very well equipped to take your money. Whether or not you get a quality education is not their responsibility.

Another little secret is that it is estimated that 90% of the jobs today do not require four years of education. Add to that that futurists estimate the average high school graduate will have more than seven careers during their lifetime and that three of those careers haven't even been invented yet. Both of these tidbits should bring cause and reflection to our educational pursuits. Maybe, just maybe, the ability read, reason, and communicate are equally, if not more, important for most of us going forward than an insanely expensive degree in an obscure discipline.

With the advent and rapid adoption of the ubiquitous Internet the focus on post-secondary education necessarily began to change, and significantly. *Busting the College Planning Lies* will help you be able to quantify so the true costs of a college education and to help you see alternatives to funding and obtaining a college degree. While online learning has made it possible to access education from virtually anywhere, the college scene remains an onsite phenomenon.

Students should be encouraged to look for alternative as well as hybrid approaches that can provide the socialization as well as the pedagogy necessary to educate our students of today and the future.

A major takeaway from *Busting the College Planning Lies* should be for parents and students alike to recognize that the more money spent on college, the less money most parents will be able to spend in retirement. We owe it to our parents and our children to get the most efficient education possible, with the best possible outcomes. Whether or not that includes college shouldn't be left up to the status quo.

— *Jim Kindred*

References

American Council President's Study 2017. Myth: College Sports Are a Cash Cow, American Council on Education, available online at http://bit.ly/2WQ9zTU.

Brown, Ann. The Cost Of College In The U.S. Has Skyrocketed. Have You Ever Wondered Why? moguldom.com, November 27, 2018, available online at http://bit.ly/2WRYBxt.

Bureau of Labor Statistics. CPI Inflation Calculator. Available online at http://bit.ly/2HDi6Xz.

Clark, Kim. College Board Says Tuition Rose Faster Than Inflation Again This Year, Money Magazine Online, retrieved November 4, 2015 at http://bit.ly/2WGSGeu.

Jaschik, Scott. Are Prospective Students About to Disappear? Inside Higher Ed, January 8, 2018, available online at http://bit.ly/2I2PzKw.

Kawasaki, Guy (2019) *Wise Guy*, Portfolio/Penguin: New York, NY.

Kristof, Cathy. What's Behind the Soaring Costs of College Textbooks, CBS News Online, January 26, 2018, available online at https://cbsn.ws/2WGVb0m.

Schoen, John. "Why college costs are so high and rising", CNBC.
    com, December 8, 2016, available online at https://cnb.
    cx/2HYPYO3.
The Scholarship System. The Real Reason Why College Costs Are
    So High and What You Can Do About It, April 5, 2019 avail-
    able online at http://bit.ly/2WQWDNR.
TruBirch. The Astonishing Increase In The Price Of Textbooks
    Since 2004, Visualized, Digg, March 9, 2019 available online
    at http://bit.ly/2EXb9NO.

THE PRESTIGIOUS HISTORY OF COLLEGE

It takes curiosity to learn.
It takes courage to unlearn.
Learning requires the humility to admit what you don't know today.
Unlearning requires the integrity to admit that you were wrong yesterday.
Learning is how you evolve.
Unlearning is how you keep up as the world evolves.

— Adam Grant
Author, *The Power of Knowing What You Don't Know*

THE REASON AND DESIRE for a college education have not always been for a single, homogenous goal. Like many American institutions, its purpose has morphed over time. Like the chicken and the egg, it's hard to say whether the definition of college has evolved to fit society or vice versa. However, it stands to reason that the purpose and outcome of higher education have changed, all the same.

In colonial times, a college education was often a precursor to life in the clergy. Many college institutions were founded by religious groups to better prepare their future ministers. Over time, education became more and more secular, and the college experience became something of a status symbol. Harvard, the United States' oldest, and perhaps most "elite," university graduated fewer and fewer clergymen over the centuries.

In part, this explosion of higher education can be attributed to the rise of Democracy. It was Thomas Jefferson's wish that a voting public be an educated public, and in 1862, this dream became a reality because of the Land-Grant Acts that Abraham Lincoln signed.

This made public land available for universities to build, and the number of college institutions exploded from a mere 23 in 1800 to 821 colleges by 1897.

It wasn't until the forties and fifties, however, that college education really became the "norm" for most Americans. Not only did the doors of higher education open for women at this time, but the GI Bill was also introduced. Suddenly, a college education was affordable for the middle class, accessible to most people, and college became representative of the doorway to the American Dream. The GI Bill was even called "the magic carpet ride to the middle class."[1]

So what's with the history lesson? In part, this goes to show the growing access to education in the United States, which, of course, is a good thing. However, it also highlights a glaring disparity between college education "then" and college education now. The mindset that we have carried over from the 1950s is that college is necessary to be successful. Yet, in the America we live in right now, college is not the fastest path to wealth or success. Not for everyone. We're not arguing the power or importance of an education, but rather the necessity of a degree in order to earn a liveable wage. The truth is, many of our commonly held beliefs about higher education—namely that a degree means a higher salary and guaranteed employment—are simply not true anymore.

This isn't just a theoretical problem either; it's compounded by the fact that the cost of education is not what it used to be. If you're young, you've probably heard stories from grandparents who were able to pay for an entire year of college by working through the summer. It's easy to be nostalgic for something like that, even when you haven't lived it, when you consider the alternative. Namely,

---

1 All history info: https://www.worldwidelearn.com/articles/history-higher-education/ and https://college-education.procon.org/history-of-college-education/

that education costs are rapidly outpacing inflation rates. Recent data shows that public institutions have an average annual price increase of about 1.5%, while private colleges are averaging 6.2% each year.[2] You almost have to earn the annual salary you're supposed to get from an education just to pay for one—a backwards notion compared to that of our predecessors.

The College Paradigm is Due for an Overhaul

So what do we do with this information?

The lesson here is twofold. First, depending on your definition of success and the life you wish to lead, college is not the only available path for you. Second, college is a huge financial commitment and one that deserves careful thought and attention. If your dream is to be a doctor, a lawyer, a scientist, a professor, or a librarian—among other professions—then yes, a degree is necessary. Often multiple degrees. You may even do the deep internal work and decide that college is for you, for other reasons.

To that point, we want to make all options clear to you so that you (or your children) can enter adulthood with less debt, more confidence, and a sense of purpose and fulfillment. We're here to expose and bust the modern myths of college and college planning so that your unique road becomes a bit clearer to you. Empowerment is the name of the game, and the road you walk should be one you feel inspired to take—not the one that others choose for you. And it's clear that we still live in a culture where college is pushed as the only and most necessary option.

---

2 https://educationdata.org/average-cost-of-college-by-year

THE OVERWHELMING COST
OF COLLEGE

IT'S NOT A SECRET that college is costly. Many people spend well over a decade saving for college, and it can still seem like there's not enough. Unfortunately, we're not going to burst any bubbles here... it is expensive, and maybe even more so than you think it is.

And the reality is, kids aren't always thinking about cost when they're searching for colleges. They're likely basing a lot of their decisions on other factors, including how the campus looks, and where it's located. These are of course, important factors, yet shouldn't be the primary ones. Yet kids don't receive the kind of financial education in high school that makes it possible for teens to really grasp the financial commitment of college.

Here's the thing, college costs are rising each year, as they have for a long, long time. Much of this can be attributed to inflation and institutions hoping to keep up. We're not here to speculate why colleges are raising costs, just to reiterate that they are increasing. If you don't factor inflation into your savings strategy, you could be in for a rude awakening.

So, what's the real scoop on college costs? As we mentioned

earlier, public colleges are generally increasing at a rate of 1.5% and private ones are increasing at a rate of 6.2% each year. Over the span of a year, maybe that's not so much. Your $25,000 tuition to a public university may increase by just $375. Yet what happens if you're a brand new parent opening a savings account for your child's future education? You might conduct some research and conclude that you need only save $100,000 in 18 years. That would cover things, right? If you don't know the rate at which colleges raise tuition, it's a logical conclusion.

Unfortunately, in this scenario, by the time you look into college costs again, it's likely too late to make a major course correction. It might not be until your child is looking at colleges themself that you realize that you haven't saved enough, and that's not a good feeling. Yet it's true, and it's provable with the Truth Concepts calculators.

Sending Multiple Children to College

Years ago, my husband, Todd, and I met with a client of ours who was a lawyer. He made $450,000 a year, yet had very little in his checking account to show for it. At the end of our meeting, he declared that he was going to educate his girls–all four of them. To him, this meant sending all four girls to his Alma Mater, Austin College in Sherman, Texas.

For him, it was all about legacy, understandably. His parents met there, he met his wife there, and he wanted his girls to be a part of that too. He was adamant that he would give his girls the same deal his parents gave him. He would pay for their undergrad tuition. At the time, his oldest daughter was 14, and his youngest was 8. And the cost of tuition was about $40,000 at this point in time.

The youngest girl, at 8 years, would begin college in 11 years, and finish in 4 more years. While the oldest daughter would begin school in 5 years, and attend for 4. That means that just to send the oldest to school, this attorney would only have 5 years to save for the oldest child's first year of school. Overall, he'd be saving for 14 years, to put all girls all the way through a 4-year degree.

Using the Cash Flow calculator from Truth Concepts, we can actually show exactly how much it will cost. In the calculator, we will just illustrate out to 14 years, and use 3 Cash Flow columns to show each of the girls' tuition costs. At the time of this example, we used an inflation rate of 7% to show the increasing cost, which was accurate for Austin College at the time of the illustration.

We've isolated each of the tuition time-frames, so that you only see the cost while each daughter is in attendance.

What this calculator shows is the cost of tuition in each year, which would be $52,000 by the time the attorney's oldest girl begins college. In the final year of the 8-year-old's degree, tuition would be $96,394. Over the entire time-frame, this is $1,153,828 spent on college.

See Chart 1, next page.

This is the moment where the attorney almost fell off his chair. In his mind, $40,000 a year wasn't much to blink at with his salary. Despite having a bare bones checking account, and very little to work with. Yet that's not the end. We also had to consider how much money he'd have to have today in order to make all of this happen.

Since the attorney didn't have anything to work with, we decided to reverse engineer the problem. Essentially, we decided to simulate an account earning 4% net each year without annual contributions. When doing so, that revealed the uncomfortable answer. Just to break even on his investment in his daughters, he'd have to have $817,064 socked away.

See Chart 2 on page 13.

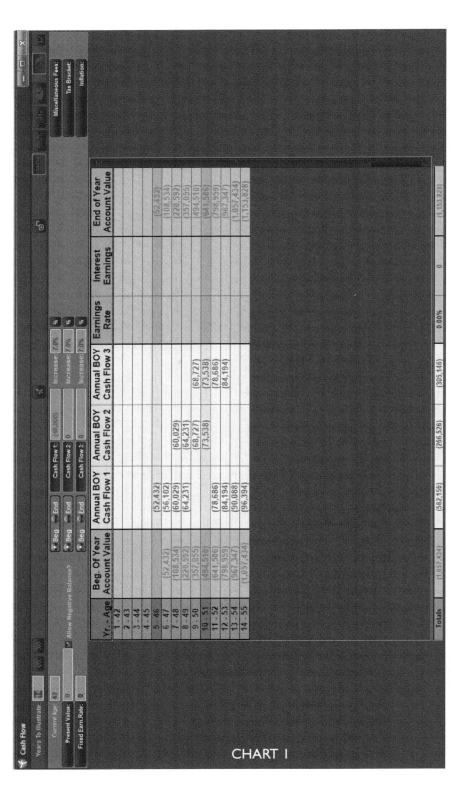

CHART I

Years To Illustrate

Current Age: 42
Automatic PV: 817,064
Fixed Earn. Rate: 4.0%

Beg / End
Beg / End
Beg / End

Allow Negative Balance?

Cash Flow 1: (40,000)   Increase 7.0%
Cash Flow 2: 0   Increase 7.0%
Cash Flow 3: 0   Increase 7.0%

Miscellaneous Fees
Tax Bracket
Inflation

Yr. - Age	Beg. Of Year Account Value	Annual BOY Cash Flow 1	Annual BOY Cash Flow 2	Annual BOY Cash Flow 3	Earnings Rate	Interest Earnings	End of Year Account Value
1 - 42	817,064				4.00%	32,683	849,746
2 - 43	849,746				4.00%	33,990	883,736
3 - 44	883,736				4.00%	35,349	919,085
4 - 45	919,085				4.00%	36,763	955,849
5 - 46	955,849	(52,432)			4.00%	36,137	939,554
6 - 47	939,554	(56,102)	(60,029)		4.00%	35,338	918,790
7 - 48	918,790	(60,029)	(64,231)		4.00%	31,949	830,680
8 - 49	830,680	(64,231)	(68,727)	(68,727)	4.00%	28,089	730,307
9 - 50	730,307		(68,727)	(73,538)	4.00%	23,714	616,566
10 - 51	616,566		(73,538)	(78,686)	4.00%	18,780	488,269
11 - 52	488,269	(78,686)	(78,686)	(84,194)	4.00%	13,236	344,132
12 - 53	344,132	(84,194)			4.00%	7,030	182,774
13 - 54	182,774	(90,088)			4.00%	3,707	96,394
14 - 55	96,394	(96,394)			4.00%	0	0
Totals	96,394	(582,156)	(266,526)	(305,146)	0.35%	336,765	0

CHART 2

The calculation isn't meant to deter anyone from pursuing an education. Rather, it's to help encourage more families to think seriously about the cost of a college education. It's not just something you or your kids should do because the neighbors are doing it, or it's part of the family legacy. There must be a bigger WHY.

Looking at It from a Different Angle

There are numerous ways to pick apart the cost of college. The previous example exposes the reality of saving "too little, too late," as well as saving for big families. However, there are other ways to think about the cost of college. Is saving for one student, far in advance, less expensive? Not necessarily, thanks to the inflation piece. However, it definitely makes an impact on how much you must earn or put away to reach your benchmark.

This time, let's use the Education calculator from Truth Concepts. Let's just enter the following information: the current tuition of $25,000, the annual increase of 7%, the child's age, and expected start and finish dates. Below, you'll see that by the time your child actually starts school, tuition is $52,621. If they finish school in four years, their final year of school, tuition will cost $64,463. Cumulatively, that's $233,636 to pay for school. So if you were under the impression you'd only need to save about $100,000 for school, you'd be more than a bit behind.

See Chart 3 next page.

Then, of course, what happens if your child decides they'd rather go to Harvard? As of writing, Harvard's tuition is $54,000. By the time your child turns 18, the first year's tuition could be $113,662. Over four years of school, that's a cumulative cost of $504,653. While this may seem like an extreme example, this is what the data suggests is possible in the future. Since we can't know for

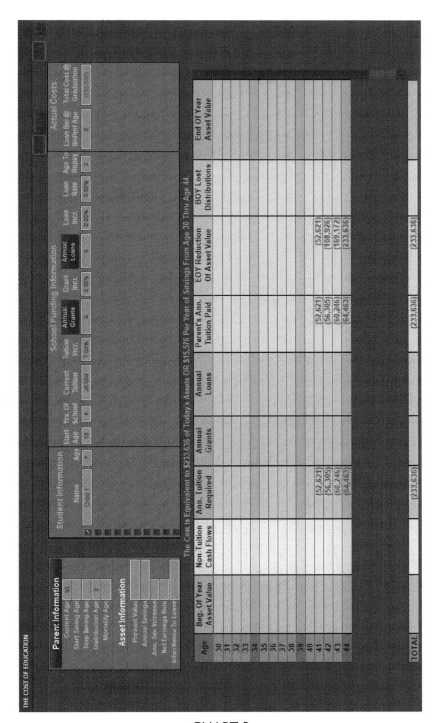

CHART 3

sure until it happens, this number is as real a prediction as it gets based on our current reality. And chances are, you didn't think it necessary to save over $500,000 in under 20 years.

See Chart 4, next page.

What may be more sobering? This illustration only covers the tuition. College costs also include housing, textbooks, meal plans, parking fees, and much more. There's a lot that goes into a college education, and it's a massive undertaking to save money for this excursion.

How Soon is Too Soon to Share with Your Kids?

While the cost of college may seem like a burden for parents to bear alone, there can actually be great benefits to teaching this information to your children. The question is, how soon? Schools lack much of the fundamental financial education necessary to make major financial decisions, like college. Yet, students are asked to make these decisions anyway. And whatever you cannot pay in cash, grants, and scholarships must usually be paid in loans. Teens are signing these loans without a good understanding of how much they're really signing up to pay, and how long they might be paying it. Most kids have limited experience with paying bills and managing money.

The sooner you can teach financial responsibility, the better. That doesn't mean you must have the college cost discussion right away. Instead, you may consider how you can help your kids learn about managing money from a young age. Not only can this help them learn financial responsibility, it has the added benefit of preventing a sense of entitlement.

Younger kids can benefit from an allowance system to save money for purchases that they want beyond basic needs. Older

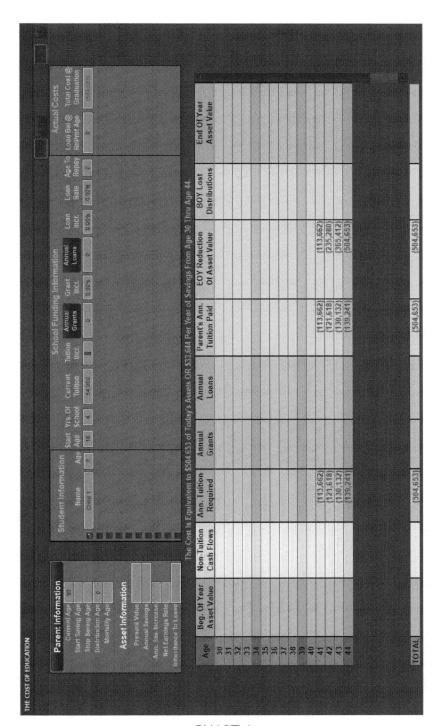

CHART 4

teens can benefit from getting a job to finance things like a car, a phone, or other purchases. And in that sweet spot, where kids are entering high school, it can be helpful to have them start thinking more seriously about college and what it can cost—both them and you, the parent.

DIVING INTO
OPPORTUNITY COST

RAISING YOUR CHILDREN with a sense of financial responsibility and knowledge doesn't just prepare them for college. It
also helps them to understand Opportunity Costs. Because really,
saving for college doesn't just impact the parents or the kids on an
individual level, it also impacts the whole family over the course of
this savings period.

When you, the parent, are saving for anything, that money can
no longer be used for something else. That money can't be spent at
home, or on vacations, or making memories in the present. There
may be other money in the equation, or the cost may be worth it to
everyone, yet it's important to understand that there is a cost. If you
don't have these difficult, often emotional, conversations with your
children, you don't give them the chance to understand and make
more intentional financial decisions on the topic itself.

Having this discussion, in different ways and at different stages
in your child's life also gives your children the chance to take ownership of their education. It may help them to seek more funding,
study harder, and work to ease the costs wherever possible. And

this is critical—your kids SHOULD be invested in their education if that's what they choose to do.

Defining Opportunity Cost

Opportunity cost can best be defined as the financial implications of one financial decision over another. This cost can feel invisible, and the Education Calculator brings it to the foreground so you can see the real implication.

Here's the thing—your money is finite. It's why you save for things like college in the first place, to accumulate enough over time. The other major event people typically save money for, on this scale, is retirement. (Though we cover some of the downfalls in the current retirement paradigm in the book Busting the Retirement Lies.) Yet every dollar put toward one account, typically, is a dollar your other accounts don't benefit from. The two "solutions" would be to either divide savings among two accounts, getting less impact with each, or wait to save for retirement until AFTER your child graduates. And in the illustration we've been using, assuming you're 30 years old today, that means waiting until age 45 to start saving.

Let's look at the implications of Opportunity Cost, and simply see what that money spent on college would become if saved at 4% until a typical retirement age of 65. All we're doing is including a savings rate. And what we see is that while the cumulative cost of college would be $233,636 for four years, that money could have become $563,335.

See Chart 5, next page.

If you assume a mortality age of 90, that's over $33,000 a year in retirement income lost. The tendency in college planning is to think solely about the money spent now. Yet what you do with your

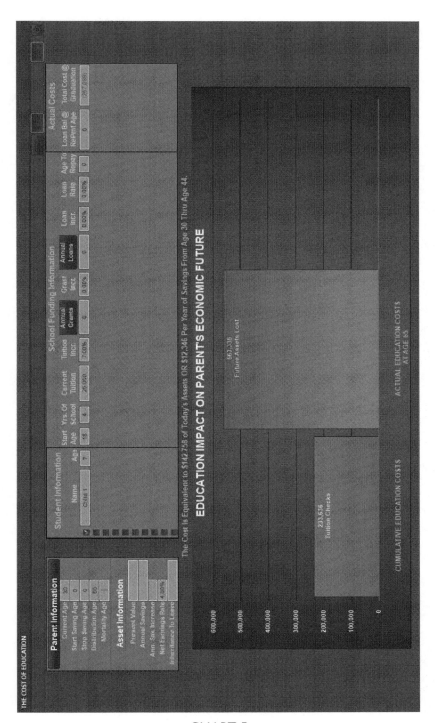

CHART 5

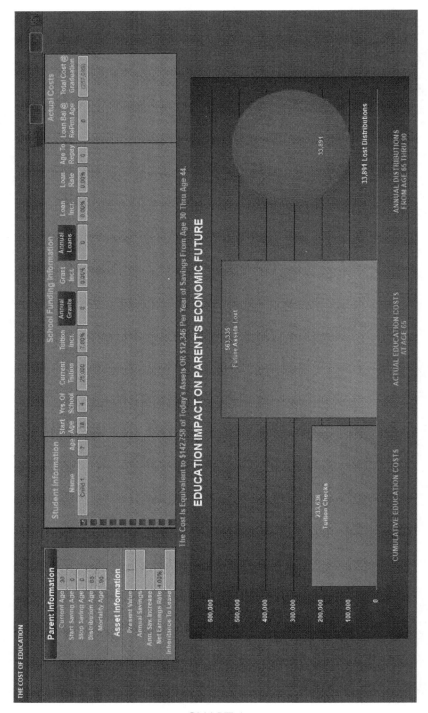

EDUCATION IMPACT ON PARENT'S ECONOMIC FUTURE

The Cost Is Equivalent to $142,758 of Today's Assets OR $12,346 Per Year of Savings From Age 30 Thru Age 44.

CHART 6

money now affects what you can or cannot do in the future, and that's critical to consider..

See Chart 6 on page 24.

We can prove this by working backwards with the calculator. The calculator shows that with $142,758 dollars today, earning 4% and being left alone, you could have half a million dollars by age 65. Withdrawing that money for college eliminates this potential.

See Chart 7, next page.

You cannot recoup those lost dollars spent on college. You must decide if it's worth it, and think about how to alleviate the financial load.

Opportunity cost seems theoretical because you don't really have a tangible way to know what you've "lost." However, in this case, it's clear: when you interrupt your compounding interest, you lose major savings. When you pay for college, you lose major future potential.

Storing cash in a whole life insurance policy, rather than a 529 plan or Qualified Plan is a step in the right direction. We'll get into that more in-depth in the next chapter, however, the most compelling reason is that you can use a life insurance policy to finance anything (no restrictions) without losing the power of compounding interest. This means you don't have to have an either/or savings scenario, or lose half a million dollars of retirement funds to send your child to school.

The Possibilities of Future Assets

Let's look at the issue in a different way. What happens if the attorney from earlier had the $817,000 in an account? Let's say he was earning the same 4% rate. In the 23 years it takes him to reach age 65, his assets would be over $2 million. That's if he just left the account untouched.

See Chart 8 on page 27.

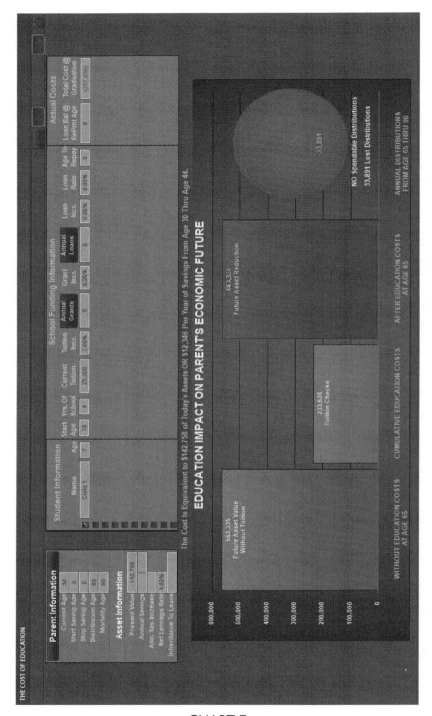

EDUCATION IMPACT ON PARENT'S ECONOMIC FUTURE

The Cost Is Equivalent to $142,758 of Today's Assets OR $12,346 Per Year of Savings From Age 30 Thru Age 44.

CHART 7

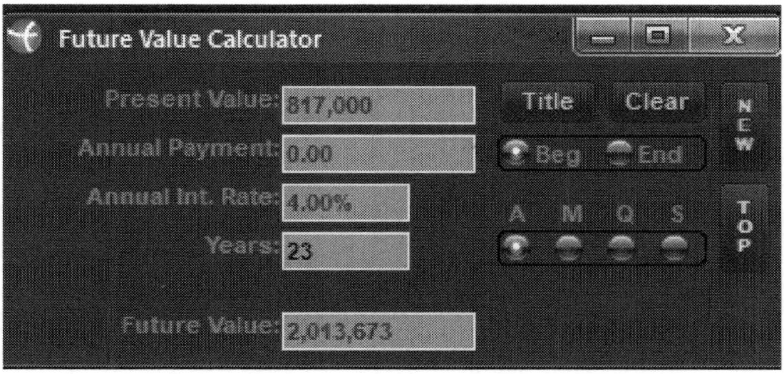

CHART 8

Remember: the alternative was spending down that money in 14 years to send all his girls to school. Now, at this point, he could use this $2 million and change for income distributions. Cash flow, ultimately, is what's important during this stage of life, because cash flow pays the bills. Net worth is simply a fun fact.

If we put the $2 million into a Payment calculator, let's see what happens. In the calculator (*Chart 9, below*), $2 million is represented as "Present Value" because at age 65, that's how much will be in the account. The "Future Value" is 0 because he is going to pay down the account. The account can keep earning 4%, and for this example let's say he plans to pay down the account to age 90, so over 25

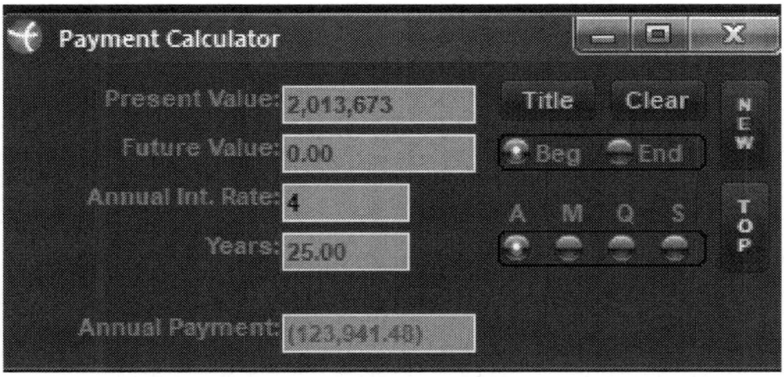

CHART 9

years. The result is $123,941 of income each year.

If the attorney pays down the account to send his girls to college, he loses about $124,000 in annual income during retirement. We showed this to the attorney, too, and he actually teared up.

What he said was, "You know, I have another brother that's an attorney, and a brother that's a physician, and I have a sister that's got three or four PhDs, because our deal with our parents was as long as we maintain the grades, we can have as much schooling as we want. The last few years of my parents' lives, my two brothers and I had to support my mom and dad, and I resented every check I wrote for the poor job my dad did with his finances. I didn't realize until today what we cost them."

We all make decisions with our money that we think will lead to the most desirable outcome. This is not meant to scare anyone away from getting an education. However, it's a call to wake up and be more intentional about the money you spend. If parents can help their teen and young adult children understand this as they enter high school and college, it can be a great incentive to think more wisely about where they're going to school, why they're going, and if school is even the best possible fit.

THE PITFALLS OF SAVING
FOR COLLEGE

Myth #1: A 529 Plan is the Best Way to Save for College

When it comes to college "planning," saving for college is one of the biggest hurdles for parents and young teens alike. There's no avoiding the truth that college is expensive—more expensive than it used to be, and as we mentioned in Chapter One, costs are only increasing.

Many parents choose to start saving for college when their children are young, in the hopes that by the time those children are 18, there will be plenty of funds. This, of course, is a well-meaning strategy. In fact, it's the practical strategy for hopeful parents and one that by all rights provides more options for children than NOT saving.

The problem, however, is the method of saving. Many Americans are led astray by financial planners and typical advice to save into a 529 plan or other education funds. These accounts are meant to function as a dedicated investment fund exclusively for education costs. And therein lies the rub—these accounts are subject to the whims of Wall Street, and have no flexibility.

Here's the thing. 529 plans are a limited-time investment. Unlike other investments, 529 plans have about an 18-22 year shelf life. They're designed to fund college and associated costs, and that's pretty much it. If the stock market goes down, like it did in the 2008 recession, there's not adequate time for recovery. Parents who had already dedicated years of savings into 529 plans saw funds plummet practically overnight. It can take years for a stock market account like this to recover from financial strain, and the one thing a 529 plan doesn't always have is time. What happened to students due to start college in 2009? This system of saving into a 529 or other investment account is that there really isn't much saving happening when you look at the long term. They're just gambling disguised as saving.

There Are Other, More Flexible Ways to Save

So you may be wondering, what IS a good way to save for college? Our answer would be dividend-paying whole life insurance with a mutual insurance company. It's a mouthful, yet each word matters. First, let's break down what dividend-paying whole life insurance is. This type of life insurance offers permanent coverage, in addition to a cash value component. The cash value is a savings element that is not correlated to the stock market, and in addition to growing through premium payments, it also earns   dividends. The reason it grows is because when you work with a mutual company, policy owners are partial owners of the company. As a partial owner, you get to partake in a portion of all profits.

Saving into a whole life insurance policy allows you to save automatically and systematically. You can even put premiums on auto-pay, like a bill, to ensure that your policy stays in force and your cash value grows. Your cash value cannot decrease because performance is not based on the stock market. When the company profits, you get to partake in some of those profits in the form of dividends, which you can use to buy additional paid-up insurance to grow your cash value.

Whole life insurance is also a liquid asset, which means that you can access it at any time, for any reason. The most efficient way to access your cash reserves is through a policy loan, although you can withdraw cash as well. Now, you may be wondering—aren't we trying to avoid college debt? And while in general, it's wise to avoid taking on too much debt, there can be a benefit to leveraging your cash. When you take a policy loan, you're really taking a loan from your life insurance company. When you do this, you use your cash value as collateral to back up the loan. This allows your cash value to continue to compound uninterrupted, while you use the insurance company's money to educate your child or yourself.. That means that your money is still growing (which is reassuring, considering loan repayment probably won't begin until after graduation).

So why take a loan from the life insurance company instead of the government? Isn't all debt the same? Well, not exactly. Here's where things get especially interesting. For starters, you can take a loan against your cash value at any time, for any reason, as long as that cash is not already up as collateral. This means that if you are saving into a life insurance policy for 18 years, and your child decides college is not for them, your money isn't locked away. Instead, your child could use that money to start a business, get into real estate, or some other pursuit.

Secondly, life insurance has flexible repayment options. When you have a federal student loan, repayment typically begins within six months of graduation. There isn't very much wiggle room on the terms, including how much the payments will be, and for how long you're repaying them. When you take a loan from the life insurance company, they set the interest rate, and the rest of the repayment terms are up to you and/or your college student. This means if your child wants some more time after college to secure their dream job, he or she can take it.

This also creates room for creativity. Say the life insurance company is charging 5% for a policy loan, and you have the opportunity for a 2% loan somewhere else. You can take the lower interest rate. Yet, if you still need some wiggle room in your repayment schedule when you graduate, you can use your policy cash to pay off the lower interest loan or make payments on the other loan. The point here is that life insurance creates options where there otherwise wouldn't be options. And one of the sad realities of student loans is that many newly minted adults don't fully understand what they're signing up for when they take on college debt. Having options can make a massive difference.

Third, life insurance is an incredibly private asset. When you have a 529 plan, you're legally obligated to report that on your FAFSA forms when applying for loans and financial aid. This actually counts "against" you in terms of the aid you or your student is eligible for. This can make a world of difference for many families and their ability to afford school. Life insurance, on the other hand, is protected from the prying eyes of the creditors, the IRS, and the government. It doesn't need to be reported on FAFSA forms in many cases, and can therefore be a great savings tool that DOESN'T disqualify you from government aid.

Other Creative Solutions

Another benefit of whole life insurance cash values, in general, is that you can get extremely creative with how you make it work for you. For example, a friend has a unique college financing story that adds entrepreneurship to the strategy.

Notoriously, housing is an incredibly expensive part of the college experience. Most tuition costs don't include room and board, and room and board can almost be as expensive as tuition. In other words, if you plan on living in the campus dorms, you can expect to pay nearly double the costs.

Yet this friend got creative with her daughter's rooming experience. Her daughter, who was a fairly responsible, confident young woman, knew she wanted an apartment living situation. Instead of having her daughter pay rent toward nothing, she used her life insurance policy to help her finance a duplex. Then, her daughter vetted friends and other students to live with her or next to her. Everyone's rent contributed to the mortgage of the duplex, and everyone ended up saving money either on rent or the cost of living on campus.

As an added bonus, this acquaintance's daughter learned valuable skills about home ownership and renting that would translate to her post-graduate life. Her mother had peace of mind knowing that she lived in a good area and with good people. It was a win all around. This is just one example, and you can replicate it in any number of ways. The point is that if you see a creative solution, don't be afraid to implement it. It may lead to extraordinary circumstances.

To recap, life insurance can help you save because:
- The premiums show up like a bill, forcing the savings habit as a verb
- The cash is stored more safely than in banks, creating savings as a noun

- There is no tax on the growth of the cash value, enabling more efficiency
- When dividends are paid (as has been the case for most insurance companies for well over 100 years), the growth is higher than savings accounts, creating more effectiveness
- The borrowing ability (versus just withdrawing) enables the cash value to be used, paid back, used (borrowed) again, paid back again, and on and on for one's entire life
- You can use your cash when you want to, without losing out on the power of compounding interest, creating a buffer against Opportunity Costs

For more information about whole life insurance works, check out my other books: *Live Your Life Insurance* and *Busting the Life Insurance Lies*. Both have detailed information about how whole life insurance works.

CUTTING COSTS WITHOUT CUTTING VALUE

Without vision, we cannot hope to see our goal, and not seeing our goal we cannot hope to progress in the right direction.

— Mary Kimball Morgan
Founder, Principia College

BY NOW, YOU LIKELY get the idea: college is expensive. However, if your child is still committed to getting a degree and it's something he or she wants to do, don't let cost alone discourage you. Instead, consider dismantling the idea you may have been conditioned to believe: that there is a right or a wrong way to "do" college.

College comes with a lot of expectations, and young people tend to feel it from all angles. Many parents have notions about "good" schools and "bad" schools, or a love for their alma mater that they'd like their child to adopt. Media portrays college as the natural progression of a young adult's life and often paints ivy leagues and party schools as the place to be. Students also pick up on what their peers, teachers, and guidance counselors are saying. In short, there's a lot of feedback about the right schools to go to or the right order of operations.

If you're a student, know this: the only "right" answer, of course, is what you believe you want out of your post-high school life. (But more on that later.)

Aside from personal preference, there isn't a one-size-fits-all way to approach college. Yet it's this mindset that prevents many young students from getting the education that they want...in an affordable way. Normalizing alternatives to the "4-year-experience" can go a long way in trailblazing affordable college options.

For the remainder of this chapter, we want to focus on students and some cost-cutting options they may have. Parents, while this whole book is suitable for your children to read, this chapter is a particularly good one to share with your children as they consider their options.

Myth #2: You Have to Get a 4-year Degree

This may be one of the most pervasive myths about college when it comes to "right vs. wrong." A 4-year undergraduate degree is held on a pedestal and many kids are encouraged to aim for this, without realizing that it's not the only way to do things.

One example is the Associate's Degree. This is a 2-year degree that is available at community colleges, as well as many state colleges. This option is great for students who:

- Are unsure whether college is the right step, yet want an education
- Want a bachelor's degree someday, and don't yet know what kind of degree they want
- Have a desire to get a degree at a lower cost
- Want more training at an affordable cost

An Associate's Degree gives young adults more training and college experience and can look great on resumes when seeking a job while saving two years' worth of tuition costs. These degrees open doorways to many careers, too, that require more than a high school education and less than a Bachelor's Degree. Many healthcare jobs, for example, are available to those who earn an

Associate's degree. There are even opportunities in Agriculture, Information Technology, Education, and Skilled Trades that only require an Associate's degree to get started.

An additional benefit to earning an Associate's Degree at a Community College is that the cost is significantly lower. At a community college, the average annual tuition for a 2-year degree is about $3,570. At a private institution, the average cost is $14,587 a year. Either way, costs are significantly lower than a typical 4-year degree, which usually starts around $10,000 to $20,000 a year.[3] These are significant savings annually and cumulatively.

It gets even better—if you earn your Associate's Degree, you can carry it over to a four-year degree at most institutions. And because you've earned a degree, all of your credits must transfer and count toward your Bachelor's degree. (Because if you didn't know, when transferring from one college to another, some of your completed credits CAN be denied if your new school doesn't offer a comparable course.)

Here's the caveat: if you earn an Associate's in, say, nursing and then decide that you would like to get your Bachelor's in English, things can get sticky. You might get credit for all of your courses, however, every college has their own structure of required credits for each degree. While you may not have to add any general education courses to your roster in this instance, you may find yourself having to take more major-specific courses, which can add time to your degree. But if you're serious about your new major, this may be a moot point for you. Either way, you've still likely saved yourself some major money on your degree.

Just Take Courses
In some instances, you may not be seeking a degree at all. We're not

3   https://bit.ly/3DuCDZJ

ones to tell you what you should or shouldn't do. We're just here to reiterate that you have more options than you'd think. Maybe you have an idea for a career path you'd like to take that doesn't require a degree, yet you still desire education beyond your high school diploma. It's entirely possible for you to take classes tailored to your interests, without the goal of a degree.

There are several ways you can achieve this. The first method is auditing. Auditing courses allow you to sit in on classes of interest to you, without enrolling as a full-time student. You earn no grade, certificate, or credit, yet you are not required to complete course-work or take tests. You simply get to benefit from taking the class. You just have to break the mindset that a grade or certificate is the only proof of your achievement. (Though often colleges will pro-vide proof that you sat in on the course, which may benefit you.)

While you still have to pay to sit in on classes that you audit, you can put together a more piecemeal curriculum for yourself of courses you're interested in. For example, maybe you're an artist and budding entrepreneur, and you'd like a way to hone your skills or brush up on your art history. You could audit some art courses at your local community college, and maybe some econ classes, so you can develop your artistic voice. This might just be the perfect way for you to acquire skills to launch your own fine art business.

Myth #3: You Have to Take General Education Courses

Your college may think of general education courses as necessary, yet they often bear no relation to your degree and can consume up to a year's worth of courses depending on your college's require-ments. These courses can contribute to a well-rounded perspective, yet many students find them to be tedious. Here's the trade secret:

you don't always have to take general education courses if you prepare ahead of time.

Take Advanced Placement Courses

In high school, students have the option to take AP courses that offer the possibility of college credit—emphasis on the word possibility. These courses are often available beginning in Sophomore year, and students typically need a history of achievement and teacher recommendation to get into these courses. If you are a young student or have a young student, this is worth considering. It means probably needing to be in Honors classes freshman year, which means making good grades in middle school.

However, once in AP courses, students have the option at the end of the year to take an AP exam. These exams are tailored to the subject of each course and are standardized across the country. So students taking an AP World History exam in California are taking the same exam as students in Vermont. AP exams last for several hours, and are proctored like SATs; meaning, there are strict guidelines. However, success on the AP exam means potential college credit. (Note: You can pass the class, yet if you fail the exam, you do not get any college credit, and vice versa.)

That's right, even scoring well on the exam does not guarantee college credit. For starters, AP exams are scored out of 5. A score of 3 is a passing score, yet not all schools award credit for a score of 3. Most colleges will award credit for a 5, yet a score of 5 can be difficult to accomplish. Plus, all colleges have different degree requirements as well as unique course catalogs. If there is not a comparable course to an AP credit, empty credit hours may be rewarded.

I (Elizabeth) experienced this in college—I was awarded 3 credit hours per successful AP exam, which counted toward my general degree requirement of 120 credit hours. Yet, none of these credits counted for general education courses. It didn't make them useless, though, as I didn't have to pad my course load each semester.

Note: While there is no cost to enroll in an AP course, there is a cost to take the exam, which is around $100. You are not required to take the exam if you are enrolled in an AP course, which means you can opt-out if you are not confident in your ability to pass. However, it's usually advisable to take the exam, since $100 for a class-worth of college credit is much cheaper than a typical college course.

Take Dual Enrollment Courses

Dual-enrollment courses are similar to AP courses, with a key difference: they offer guaranteed college credit. Rather than a standardized exam, dual-enrollment courses are partnerships with local colleges or universities. When you take a dual enrollment course, you are effectively enrolled in a college course from the comfort of your high school. (Though sometimes you may travel or take the course online.) The coursework is likely to be more difficult than your average high school class, yet so long as you pass the course, you earn the credit.

Dual-enrollment courses, however, can be harder to come by. Not all schools offer these dual-enrollment classes, though you may be able to request them. If you can, prioritize dual-enrollment courses, since they offer real college credit. There's often a cost associated with a dual enrollment course, though usually at a "discounted" rate.

It's also important to note that while dual enrollment offers you real college credit, the credit is awarded to you at the college your school partners with. That means that there is a possibility that the credits may not transfer directly to other schools. The likelihood of your credits being accepted decreases as you move to out-of-state institutions. However, if you have your sights set on a local college, or even the college where you're enrolled for the course, getting the credit can be worth it.

I (Elizabeth) took a dual enrollment course in high school, and earned credit at the college I attended that fall. The course counted as one of my Science general education courses and made it that much easier for me to focus on my major requirements.

Test Out of General Education Courses Completely

This may be the best-kept secret of all: CLEP exams.

Like AP exams, CLEP is run by the College Board. These exams operate on a pay-per-course basis and allow young students to test out of and earn credit for college courses. These exams can save you thousands of dollars and potentially a few semesters of school. The idea is that you can pay a fraction of the cost of a course to skip straight to the exam portion. If you pass, you earn that college credit. You can use this to complete general education courses and potentially even skip the introductory courses for your major. This allows students to jump right into the advanced coursework for their degree. This is both a time saver and a money saver, meaning that you can graduate early and launch your career.

CLEP exams are also shorter than AP exams. AP exams are usually a 3 or 4-hour test, while CLEP exams typically work like your normal semester final. These tests are about one to two hours. Unless there's a written portion to the exam, test results are immediate, so you know if you've earned the credit or not. And, you don't have to take a course to take the exam. Now, it's recommended that you study for your exams, of course (you are paying for them), yet you can skip any busy work that may have been assigned in a semester.

This may potentially be a good way to earn credit for a course you don't wish to take, yet are required to have. Or, to retest for a course you did not pass or complete, without paying for that course all over again. To reiterate: this is not a less expensive way to take a COURSE, it is simply a way to test OUT OF a course. If there's a topic you wish to delve deeper into and really experience, it's ideal to take the course.

If you have concerns about the impact of testing out of courses, don't write off CLEP exams just yet. It turns out that CLEP exams have actually improved graduation rates for undergraduates who may typically struggle in a college environment by 5.5%. CLEP has also correlated to better overall GPAs and better course performance in more advanced courses. Getting a degree is hard work, and knowing what tools are available to help you succeed can make the difference between earning the degree or not. There's no shame in passing out of some courses that might otherwise cause stress, frustration, or boredom. College is meant to serve YOU, and further your education, so don't believe that you can't make it work for you.

As of writing, there are 34 exams across multiple topics. All CLEP exams are $89 and cover a wide variety of introductory college courses. It's also worth noting that if you're in the military, you can take CLEP exams for free. Here are some tips before enrolling in a CLEP exam:

- Find out where your nearest exam site is, which may impact when you schedule your exam.
- Cross-check which colleges accept CLEP credit against the colleges you wish to enroll in. This may impact where you apply to school, or whether you want to take certain exams. You can search for college CLEP policies by location or name from the CLEP site (clep.collegeboard.org).
- Note your school's (or potential school's) CLEP policies,

including accepted exams, required exam grades, and credit hours awarded.

- If you know the school you're attending, you can start taking your exams based on your degree requirements and your school's CLEP policy. If you do not yet know where you are attending, you can use CLEP policies and your school's degree requirements as a guideline for where you might get the most impact from CLEP exams.
- Download study materials for your exam and make sure you're prepared. You can buy a complete study guide that contains materials for all 34 exams, or purchase study materials for each exam individually. On the CLEP website, you can also find free resources like study guides and suggested learning platforms.
- Schedule your test!

Myth #4: Scholarships and Grants Aren't Feasible

It's true, to a degree, that applying for scholarships and grants can feel like a time-consuming activity with little return. However, that doesn't mean it's a fruitless activity altogether. It's mostly a matter of barking up the right tree. If you spend all of your time applying for small scholarships that are difficult to get, you might not be making the best use of your time.

Instead, focus your efforts on scholarships and grants that are of higher value and also have narrower qualifications. For example, a $500 scholarship for an essay on optimism that anyone can apply for might seem like an easy get. However, you're competing against a WIDE pool of people (potentially ALL college-aged students) for a very broad topic. Ditch Scholarships.com and get a little more creative with your search parameters.

First things first, start local. Around freshman year of high school, get with the guidance counselor and ask what kind of awards, scholarships, and grants are available through the school. If you've ever attended a high school graduation or awards ceremony, you know what this is about. While many awards are not monetary, some are. The problem is, the school rarely broadcasts these opportunities—and it's hard to try and qualify for something you don't know anything about. Guidance counselors can typically supply you with what kinds of awards the school offers, and how to be eligible. As you'd expect, they tend to hover around academic achievement (sometimes general, sometimes for specific subjects), athletic achievement, musical accomplishment, and character development. TRIO counselors can also be a good resource, which represents Federal aid programs on a needs basis.

Now, it's time to open up your search from local to state-wide. That's right—each individual state boasts its own grant and scholarship programs. Just search your state grant agency to see what's available. For example, in Illinois, many grants are awarded to children of military families or other public service members. While you're at it, you may want to research federally available scholarships and grants.

Next, you'll want to widen your search a little bit more. There are many grants and scholarships available from charities, organizations, and other groups committed to serving certain demographics. For example, you may qualify for religious-based aid through your church. There are many grants and scholarships available to young women looking to go into STEM or other male-dominated fields. You may even find money for aspiring film students, young activists, budding writers, children of service workers, and so much more.

Consider who you are, what makes you unique, and the passions you hold...then get to researching. You won't know until you dig in whether there is a scholarship or grant tailored perfectly to who you are and what you represent.

Finally, ask your school what kind of programs they have. Most Colleges have programs to provide funding to students. Sometimes, the money is set aside for in-state students, sometimes it is set aside for high GPAs or rising athletic stars. Other times, schools have money available for students who exemplify passion or leadership skills. You might find that there are more funds available to private colleges, simply because they have a strong donor base (however, they tend to have higher tuition than public colleges).

When it comes to scholarships, focus less on quantity and more on quality. Otherwise, you run the risk of spreading yourself too thin. Apply to programs catering to a niche that you're a part of. You may feel like there's more competition this way, yet in reality, it's likely there's less competition...you're just up against more qualified applicants. Focus on standing out and putting your all into what you submit.

KNOW THYSELF!

Myth #5: College is Where You Should Find Yourself.

Many people elect to find themselves in college. We won't argue the importance of finding yourself (after all, finding what makes you happy is one of the secrets to Prosperity). However, using college as a self-assessment is an incredibly expensive way to accomplish that. Do you have to have your whole life figured out in order to make college a worthwhile experience? Of course not, it would be impressive if you did. However, you may want to put some serious thought into:

What you want to GET from your college experience

The career path you feel is right for you

What path is going to take you where you want to go in the most efficient and affordable way.

This isn't just a nice sentiment——it's an exercise in maturity. You're making an investment into your future, your career. Is the path you're choosing going to have the results you want (i.e. good income, your dream job, etc.)? The harsh truth is that college is not for everyone. These results might be easily accomplished with a degree in hand, yet that's the thing...you'll need the degree. The harsh truth is that college completion statistics are pretty grim. More than a million college students dropout of college every year. Less than half of college students graduate "on-time."[4] These are just a few of the sobering statistics.

This isn't meant to scare, it's simply to paint a picture. College is difficult, and it's not for everyone. While the exact reasons for dropout rates may be unquantifiable (at least, to a precise degree), some things are clear. Namely, one reason it takes some students so long to complete college—sometimes 6 or more years for a 4-year degree—is due to a lack of self-knowledge. When you change college majors, your graduation requirements are overhauled. This means that many of the courses you take may be rendered "void." For example, if all of your credits are in English courses, and you realize your passion is Chemistry, those credits don't transfer well. You may have just tacked on a few years to your degree.

Life happens. It's not the end of the world if this happens to you. However, you can reduce this possibility by entering college with a good idea of your trajectory. That way, the chances of you changing your mind later are drastically reduced. Sometimes, you may find that there's simply a better path to your dream career than you realized. For example, say your dream is journalism, so you go into school seeking an English degree. If in your Sophomore year you realize that a Mass Communication degree is a better fit, you might lose fewer requirements than a complete discipline change.

In some families, there can be a lot of pressure to go to college and figure things out, yet that can lead to a directionless education or eventual dropout. And unfortunately, you have to pay those

---

4 https://www.forbes.com/sites/markkantrowitz/2021/11/18/shocking-statistics-about-college-graduation-rates/?sh=132e826d2b69

loans whether you graduate or not. If you're unsure of your direction in college and beyond, there might be value in spending your first year out of high school doing some exploratory work.

Learn What Drives You

The first step to finding your direction may simply be to figure out what you are passionate about. There are many methods and ways to do so—so go ahead and try them all. Here are just a few ideas of things that can help you find your passion before you commit to college:

Extracurricular activities and Elective courses—i.e., band, choir, speech and debate team, scouting programs, farm and agriculture programs, yearbook committee, the school newspaper.

Career Fairs. These can be a great opportunity to see what common career paths are, including college alternatives such as trade schools.

Volunteer and internship opportunities. While this line of work may be more common in college, high schoolers can often get internships and volunteer positions, too. Try researching organizations that care about causes and activities you are interested in.

Absorb media. Books, podcasts, news outlets, blogs, movies, and other forms of media can expose you to career paths you may never have considered.

Research degrees. Sometimes, you don't even know what kinds of degrees are possible unless you look into them. With some research, you may be able to find new and innovative degrees you never would have known about otherwise. If something catches your eye, do a bit of research about careers supported by that degree.

Self-reflection. This, of course, happens over time. You could do daily or weekly reflection about what excites you, what brings you energy, and the things you enjoy doing in your free time. You may also find aptitude tests to reveal interesting results, which can also be great for reflection (i.e.-- do you agree with the results?).

Take More Time

This work can also be done over the course of a gap year. Gap years are not for everyone. In fact, gap years have a tendency to become a gap career if you let them (which is fine, if that's what you choose). They do, however, have the power to let young adults experience what the wider world, and working, is like before committing to a school.

If a gap year sounds of interest to you, there are ways to make this work more successful. Firstly, like a year of school, it's wise to define the parameters of your gap year. Will your gap year begin and end with a typical school year? Defining this timeline is crucial to a successful gap year because it gives you room to make a decision. Otherwise, two years might pass you by and you've decided unconsciously that you'll simply continue that way. Defining when your gap year ends gives you a deadline to decide what your next step will be. That way, no matter what you choose, you can be confident that you've chosen it intentionally.

Sometimes, the parameters are defined for you. If you apply to colleges in your senior year of high school, for example, you may have a good idea of where you intend to go. In order to secure your acceptance to your school of choice, you must often make an official declaration to defer your enrollment. This lets the school know that you intend to go, in a year's time. You still have the option to un-enroll later, but this locks in your acceptance and you won't have to reapply to school.

If you don't go this route, you'll have to reapply for school at some point. Many college applications are due sometime in the fall, with decisions mailed in late spring. If you're going to be reapplying to schools during your gap year, make sure you include those deadlines in your timeline; otherwise, you might end up waiting an additional year regardless.

The final trick to a successful gap year is to do something meaningful with your time. The purpose of a gap year is typically to get real-world experience and "find yourself." For some people, traveling is the ideal method of self-discovery. For others, it's working at the family business. The idea is to do something that can expose you to your options and a career you will love. What's going to help you succeed in the long term? Take a gap year with purpose, and you're sure to come out on the other end with confidence.

Myth #6: You Have to Start College Right Away

What happens if your gap year does extend a little longer than you thought it would? Does that mean college is out of the picture for you? Surprisingly, waiting a few additional years to go to college might not be a bad thing if you're eager to save money.

While the FAFSA form is meant to help students get financial support for the school, it's a flawed system. For example, parental income and assets factor heavily into the aid a student can qualify for, however, there's a major difference between income and assets and what someone can actually afford to pay for. The average person isn't sitting on money specifically for college. This also doesn't account for students who won't receive financial support from their parents while in school.

That's where it comes in handy to be considered an "independent student." Contrary to what you might assume, this designation isn't granted based on when a student becomes financially independent. Instead, it's granted when a person reaches the age of 24. (Though other circumstances include marriage, having a dependent, being in the military, and/or being orphaned.)

At this point, students can file a FAFSA form on their own, without declaring any parent's income. Depending on your circumstances, you might qualify for a lot more aid and support because chances are, you have fewer assets. In addition, independent student status may qualify you for additional grants and support beyond just loans.

OPTIONS BEYOND COLLEGE

Myth #7: College is the only way to make good money.
The generally accepted reason that people go to college is that it positions them for better career opportunities. However, with the way things are going today, this is less than the whole truth. College can saddle you with mounting debt, many careers still want you to have experience in addition to a degree, and pay isn't always better. This isn't the case for every field, yet it certainly is for some.

Not everyone thrives in an academic setting or is meant to launch a career through a degree program. This doesn't make those who fit in this category less valuable, and we shouldn't use college education as the only measure of worth in the "workforce."

There are many options where people can thrive, and make money using skills in marketing, networking, creativity, and labor—just to name a few things. College doesn't always get you where you need to go, and it's probably not worth taking on such a Herculean debt at a young age if it's not necessary to accomplish your vision.

In fact, a Georgetown University study[5] revealed that there are 30 million jobs paying over $55,000 per year that DON'T require a college degree. According to the US Career Institute,[6] there are 80 job categories that can make a significant income without a college degree. This includes career paths such as piloting commercial flights, installation and repair experts of ALL types (think escalators, HVAC, espresso machines—you name it), and even postmasters. The world takes all types of people to function.

The Nation Needs Trade Workers

There is a massive shortage of skilled labor right now. While yes, technically all labor requires skill, what this means is that there is a shortage of people to fill the roles of highly specialized and crucial work. Trades such as plumbing, HVAC installation and repair, bricklaying, and construction work all take highly specialized knowledge that isn't taught in a formal institution. Typically, these skilled trades are taught through apprenticeships. In other words, passed on from mentor to mentee. Yet, the world will always need such roles, and it's important that the knowledge is passed down.

This shortage has become more evident as people stayed home during the 2020 covid-19 pandemic. The more time people spend at home, the easier it is to see room for home improvement. That, and the extended use of facilities can quicken some issues. In either case, one thing became evident in 2020: the influx of home repair projects and specialized skills needed made the lack of trade workers glaringly obvious.

Before you connect the dots about WHY there's a shortage, know that according to the most recent Skilled Trades in America

5   https://repository.library.georgetown.edu/handle/10822/1047862
6   https://www.uscareerinstitute.edu/blog/80-Jobs-that-pay-over-50k-without-a-degree

Report, 83% of tradespeople are satisfied with their career choice.[7] Not only are they making good money—many of them are running their own businesses, and are happy to be doing work that is meaningful and important. Just think about what the world would look like without plumbers and electricians—not great. The people who aren't passionate about the work tend to move on to other things, yet many people find their trade extremely rewarding. And that's the secret to a lasting career: love what you do.

Here's the even better news: tradespeople WANT to pass on their knowledge. The shortage has nothing to do with gatekeeping or tradespeople being stingy about the ins and outs of the work. In fact 68% of tradespeople believe that they could grow their business if they could find more people to work.

To learn a trade, you can either attend a trade school or get an apprenticeship. In either case, you're looking at a shorter timeframe than a 4-year degree, with an almost-guaranteed job at the end. Trade schools still have associated costs, however your total obligation is typically anywhere from $5,000 to $15,000 total, making it a much easier debt to swallow. With an apprenticeship, you can even get paid to learn with on the job training. Even without an apprenticeship, you may find companies (like Tesla) who will sponsor your education.

Trade work encompasses a wide variety of career paths, too. Wind Turbine Technician careers are in high demand, and the field's growth is projected to expand by 108% in the next seven years, according to the Bureau of Labor Statistics. The healthcare field has numerous apprenticeships, most of which can be completed in a year, making it a fast track to a new job. There's an increasing need for solar panel technicians as well, with many apprenticeships available.

---

7 https://bit.ly/3Bl gwbP

Here's just a quick overview of the sheer variety of skilled trades:

Electricians

Carpenters

Plumbers

Pipefitters

Construction workers

Roofers

Structural steel and ironworkers

Painters

Boilermakers

Stonemakers

Funeral directors

Hairdressers

Real estate appraisers

And so much more...

You get the idea—there's a lot of opportunities out there. If you're thinking about learning a trade, it's worth visiting the Department of Labor's website on apprenticeships, or Apprenticeship.gov. These sites can help you find and locate opportunities.

And did we mention, learning a trade is useful pretty much ANYWHERE? There's no regional limitation to where trade skills are necessary. This means if you've dreamed of moving or living elsewhere, you might just have your pick of places to go.

Earn Certificates Online

Trade school isn't the only education alternative, either. There are actually quite a few ways to learn specialized skills that are in high demand, without getting a four-year degree. For example, on the Coursera platform, you can earn business certifications from the comfort of your own home. There are certifications tailored to a wide variety of professional interests, each with its own time frame. For example, you can earn a cybersecurity certification in about 8 months through their platform. You can also earn a bookkeeping certificate in 80 hours of work, which can help you launch a fulfilling online bookkeeping business.

Earning a certificate is a great way to prove to potential employers that you are skilled in a certain niche, whether you have a degree or not. Furthermore, these certificates can give you the training and confidence you're seeking to build your own business or add to your business's offerings (more on that later). Coursera also has full online degree programs, for a less-expensive alternative.

Another reputable platform to learn new skills is Udemy and also Udacity, both of which offer individual courses and certifications in a similarly broad range. You can take one-off courses for as little as $15, which can help you improve your resume, grow your career, or expand your business offerings.

We Live in an Entrepreneurial Age!

Of course, another option is simply to launch your OWN career. Yes, it's easier said than done. Being an entrepreneur can take some serious guts and dedication. However, it's not as hard as you might imagine to make your way in the world. Some projects require resources, however, not all entrepreneurial endeavors have a high up-front cost.

For example, many entrepreneurs get their start on freelancing platforms such as: Fiverr, Upwork, and Freelancer. These platforms connect businesses seeking work that includes (yet is not limited to) website copy, graphic design, translation, animation, programming, and more. As an "entry-level" freelancer, you may not be able to charge as much money, meaning it may be a side-hustle when you start. However, as you land clients, you get to build your portfolio and your contacts. Over time, you can charge more simply because you've put in the work and gotten results for clients.

If you begin your entrepreneurial career in this way, the key is to expand your practice over time. Adding levels of service, learning more skills (maybe through Udemy, Udacity, or Coursera), and creating a fee-based pricing structure rather than an hourly wage can make a huge difference. As you hone your skills and build your practice, keep your eye out for new and interesting ways to diversify your income streams. Can you make better use of social media, develop an online course, or write a book? Staying open to possibilities can help you grow as well.

Of course, freelancing isn't the only way to start your own business. Many successful artists launch their careers through skillful use of social media and selling work through platforms like Etsy, Shopify, and other online marketplaces. In fact, TikTok is now a popular way to gain a following and grow your audience. Due to the hyper-specific algorithm of TikTok videos, even the most niche artists are reaching their audience and making money doing what they love. The possibilities for selling art are quite literally endless.

Of course, social media wouldn't be what it is today without one thing: influencers. Influencers are entrepreneurs who market themselves to a niche audience. There are influencers for art, beauty products, fitness, lifestyle products, books, pop culture, and so much more (there are even niches within niches). The problem is that breaking into the role of an influencer can be difficult. It requires passion and a lot of upfront work with no pay. Influencers often have platforms on Instagram, TikTok, and Youtube, as well as personal blogs. These are all great platforms to make content, it's just time-consuming. It can feel like a full-time job with no pay. However, with regular content, you may one day be able to build a monetized social media life. It's just advisable that you choose something you're passionate about so that in the end, it doesn't matter if you make money or not...which of course means having a career to fall back on.

Apart from these examples, there truly is an unlimited number of ways to become an entrepreneur. It may take some self-discovery and some time, but if you want to forge your own path, believe that you can.

THE TRUTH OF
LIFELONG LEARNING

"Mind is not necessarily dependent upon educational processes. It possesses of itself all beauty and poetry, and the power of expressing them."

— Mary Baker Eddy
Author of *Science and Health with Key to the Scriptures*

AS YOU CLOSE THE CHAPTER on your time in high school, let your passion guide you. There's a temptation to go to college because it seems like the singular and linear path to success. It's in all our media, it's what our parents and grandparents did, it's even what our peers do. Yet we don't, as a society, place as much emphasis on what a huge decision it truly is. Going to college is something that is going to have a decades-long impact on your life as well as the lives of your family members. It can be an overwhelmingly positive one...or not. Yet it doesn't serve the youth of today to suggest that college is the sole path to success—not when so many young working adults are struggling under the weight of loans, or struggling to find jobs that support their loan repayment.

Instead, we recommend adopting a spirit of lifelong learning. The spirit of being a lifelong learner does not depend on your degree status. It depends on your willingness to be open, flexible, and curious. Peter Diamandis knows a thing or two about lifelong learning. Peter is an entrepreneur, physician, engineer, author, and founder of the X Prize Foundation. He says, "Whether it's architecture or astrophysics, learning new things isn't just a temporary activity. It's an invaluable ritual that keeps us cognitively sharp and turns us into lifelong students."

Many people end up finding work they love by a circuitous route. Sometimes in the process of learning and discovery, your next step becomes obvious. We like to say there are many paths up the Prosperity Mountain. And there are many Prosperity Mountains! Some of them must be discovered step-by-step! This is such an important mindset to have, regardless of your post-high school plans, because it keeps you from becoming stagnant. If you want to advance your own career, here are some endeavors and habits that can help you no matter how your path in life unfolds.

Find Your Mentors

No matter what you want to do in life, there is someone out there who has walked a similar path. It could be a family member, a local business "celebrity," or an online mentor you may never meet in person. The point is that you can identify people who have the skills and experiences you wish to have, and find a way to learn from them (often by contributing to them in some way first).

If you know a relative or family friend who works in a field you're interested in, you might ask them for an informational interview. Essentially, it's your opportunity to ask them in-depth questions about their line of work, how to break into the field, and advice for hopefuls. This can also be a great opportunity to shadow someone in a line of work you're interested in. This gives you first-hand insight on what a "day-in-the-life" looks like. Maybe this mentor can give you ideas to get started, or practical critiques on how to improve your work.

Then, you have your online mentors. These are the people you may never actually meet, yet that doesn't disqualify them as your mentor. Your greatest mentors may be the ones who write books in your field, speak at conferences, and host webinars that can help you grow. Finding this type of mentor can happen organically, or you can do deliberate research to find colleagues who have walked the path you hope to travel.

Mentorship is a rich experience that allows you to expand your idea of work and business, and grow in new and unexpected ways. Whether you're just graduating high school, or entering your fourth career path, you stand to benefit from mentorship.

Identify Your Purpose

We've touched briefly on the importance of purpose, yet we think it's important to drive home. You have the potential to spend 80 more years on this earth, or more. If you don't find things that ignite a fire in you and make you want to wake up in the morning, it can feel hard to enjoy your life. This is what drives the current retirement paradigm: people are so dissatisfied with their careers that they believe they have to push through it and make it to 65 and then they can stop. This just isn't a joyful way to live life though. If you find and pursue your purpose on this earth now, you stand a much better chance at being satisfied with your daily life from age 18-65...and beyond.

Now, finding your purpose can feel like a lifelong endeavor. I don't believe that you ever truly stop learning about who you are. However, we all must make the decision to find ourselves at some point. Doing this sooner, rather than later, can save a lot of career-based heartbreak. So start learning about what makes you tick, ask yourself the deep questions, and dare to be honest about the things that excite you, regardless of what anyone else thinks.

Cultivate Your Mindset

The world is many things, yet ultimately, it's what you make of it. When you focus on the dark and scary parts of the world, you lend them prominence in your life. When you focus on the good things happening in the world, you make space for more of that. Does that mean you turn a blind eye or ignore the world's problems? No. Actually, the entrepreneurial mind is largely based in problem-solving...which means you must have an awareness of problems that exist. You do, however, have to choose to see opportunities for good to occur in any situation. Otherwise, the negative will only overwhelm and discourage. Seek the good in every situation, and solutions tend to follow.

Cultivating a mindset that helps you to seek out opportunities will serve you well at any stage in life. Because here's the thing: we all operate on our own timetables. Your best friend could get their "big break" at the age of 20, and you might still have some time to go. Yet if you lose sight of the good, of the vision you have for your life, that "big break" can feel less certain, and the road of opportunities that could lead you there might be much harder to find. The right mindset helps you to see your way through challenges and pull the opportunities seemingly out of thin air. After all, what is an opportunity if not a possibility in hiding?

Invest in Yourself

Your income may change, as will your career, yet the one thing you will always have is YOU. You are your greatest asset—your thoughts, skills, abilities, and power to create opportunities. The things that you can do are by far the most powerful tool or resource at your disposal. That's why it's critical to invest in yourself.

Let's look at it numerically, using a Maximum Potential calculator. For this example, we'll use a high-income example to illustrate the point. Below, you can see a chart that shows a $100,000 income over 30 years. And in that 30-year time frame, $3 million passes through your hands.

See Chart 10, next page.

Yet what happens if over these 30 years, your income never increases, and the cost of living does? You're either going to have to make some compromises on your lifestyle expenses, or make more money. For this example, let's say you earn 4% more each year. Suddenly, you now have just over $5.5 million passing through your hands over 30 years.

See Chart 11 on page 77.

If you could then take every penny of that income and save it at about 4.5%, you'd have just over $10 million pass through your hands over that time frame.

See Chart 12 on page 78.

What we're getting at here is that over your lifetime, a lot of money is going to pass through your hands. You may have different numbers, however the idea is the same. So doesn't it make sense to protect as much of that as possible?

First, you have to consider how much of the money that passes through your hands that you actually get to keep. If you're making $100,000 a year, you're probably paying something like 22% of that income on taxes. Not just income tax, either. We're looking at the whole gamut—state taxes, sales tax, etc. When you do this, $10 million shoots down to $8 million, even though you've only paid about $1 million in taxes.

See Chart 13 on page 79.

Some of that money simply vanished into thin air, and why? Because of the time value of money. The money can't compound

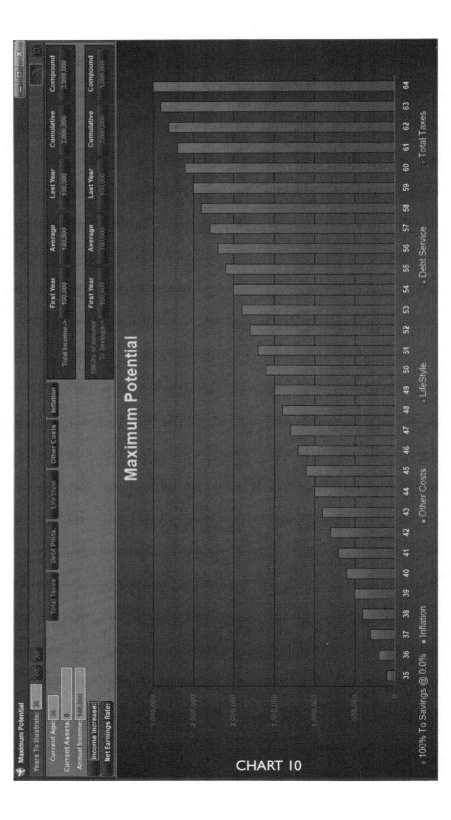

CHART 10

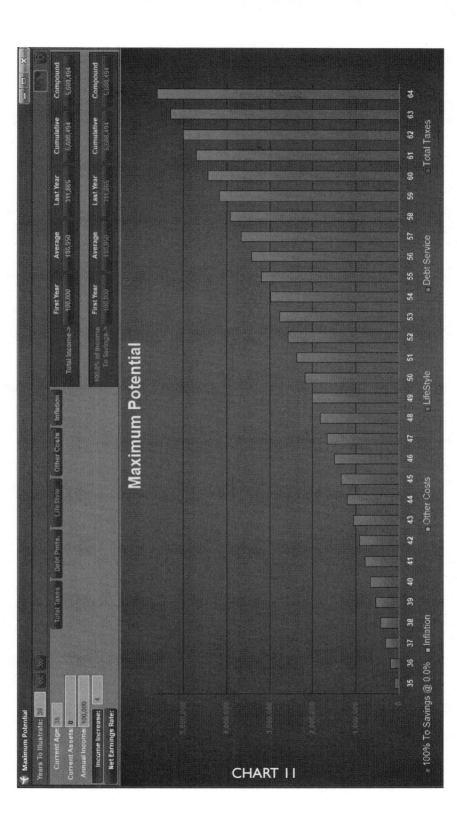

CHART 11

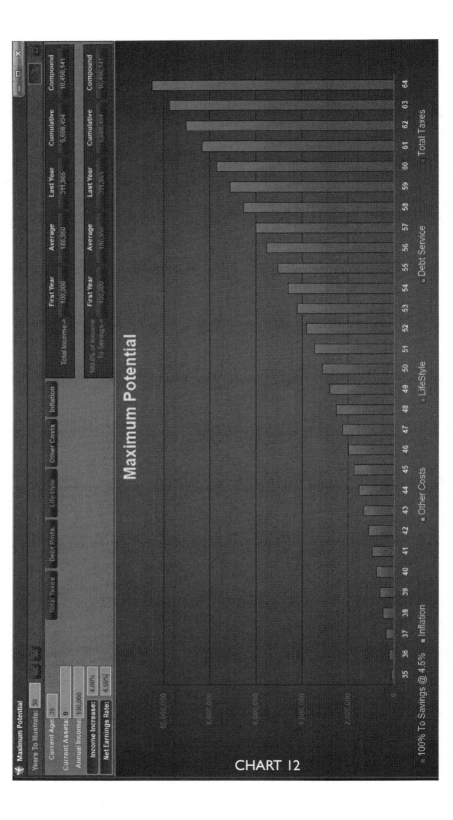

CHART 12

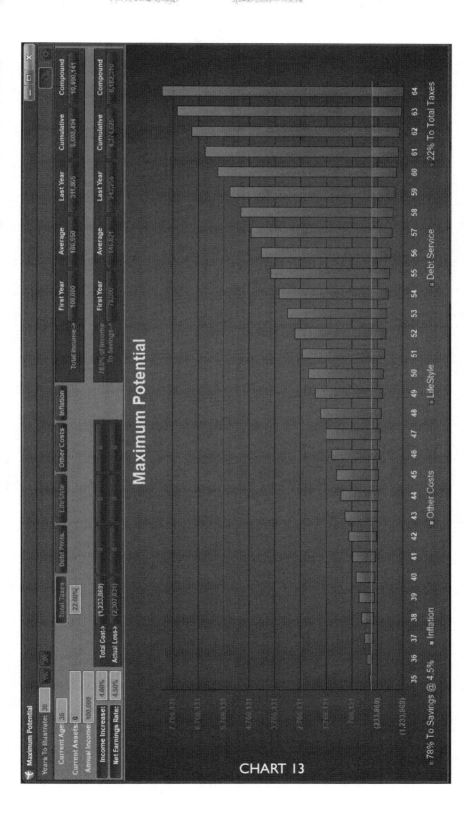

CHART 13

over time as efficiently when the money is removed from the account, making the earnings potential significantly lower.

Now, let's take debt service into account. This includes cars, homes, and credit cards. While the amount of debt may fluctuate, we can assume that about 32% of our income will go toward debt service in some way each year. Another 30% can be lifestyle, or essentially the other things you spend money on like food, clothes, and entertainment. The result? About $1.6 million available to you by the end of 30 years, despite a maximum potential of $10 million.

See Chart 14, opposite page.

Is there an answer to all this? Some might say to take on more risk by investing in the stock market. However, increasing your risk isn't increasing your chance of a home run. It's simply increasing the likelihood that you could lose more money. Even if you earned 10% on average every year, it doesn't guarantee that you will actually come out ahead. After all, an "average" still includes significant losses.

Instead, what if you could make some changes in your tax strategy and your lifestyle that helped you reduce those costs over time? The immediate impact might be small, yet on the large scale you can see significant improvement.

See Chart 15 on page 82.

When you invest a little into yourself and your lifestyle, using your own numbers, you will start to see these changes too. A vehicle like whole life insurance, for example, can be a way of "investing in yourself." Life insurance is not an investment, it's an insurance product, but ultimately that premium does two things for you. It protects your earning potential and assets via the death benefit, and it gives you an automated way to save and spend money without hurting your compounding curve. By doing this, you create options

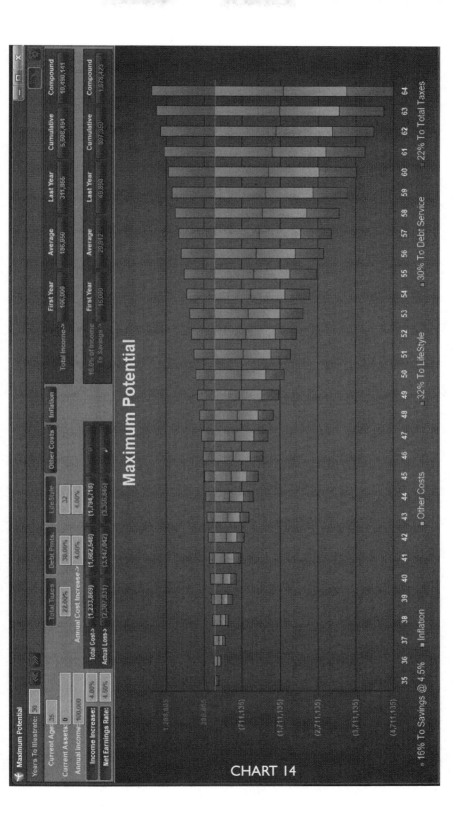

Maximum Potential

CHART 14

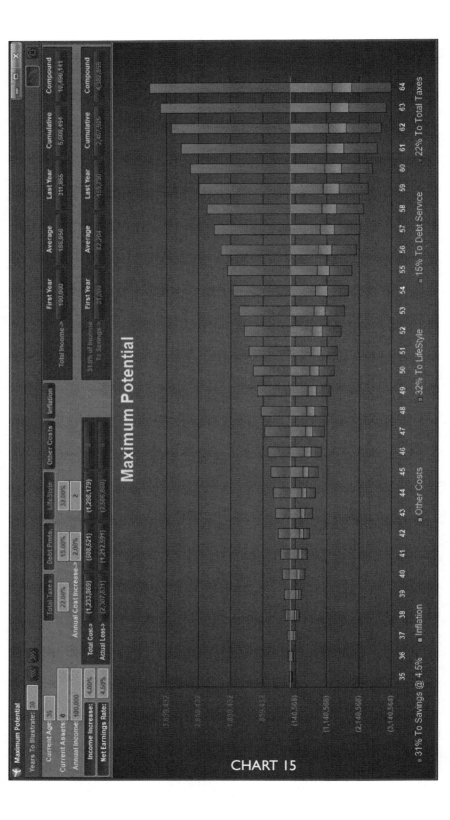

Maximum Potential

CHART 15

and opportunities to finance your life.

From an education standpoint, this is a call to invest in your own earning power. This Maximum Potential demonstration is proof that you are your best tool for earning income and saving money. No one else can do it for you. So finding the path that helps you fulfill your potential more completely, in a way that is true to you, can be a major part of fulfilling your own curve (coupled with financial products and strategies that support your endeavors). Finding your mentors, identifying your Purpose, and cultivating your mindset are all major steps in your journey that will help you see the journey through. For more ideas and ways to invest in yourself and your education, see the Resource Appendix at the back of the book.

It's Never Too Late to Become a Beginner

Regardless of your path in life, you can always be a learner. You don't have to achieve instant success by the age of 25 to be "worthy" or make an impact on the world. In fact, you can reinvent yourself at any point in time by adopting the mindset of a beginner. Whether it's your first career or your fifth, whether you're young or old, you can learn something new.

You don't have to take it from us, either. Consider all of the unconventional paths that have been taken by these trailblazers before you:

At age 23, Tina Fey was working at a YMCA.

At age 23, Oprah was fired from her first reporting job.

At age 24, Stephen King was working as a janitor and living in a trailer.

At age 27, Vincent Van Gogh failed as a missionary and decided to go to art school.

At age 28, Wayne Coyne (from The Flaming Lips) was a fry cook.

At age 30, Harrison Ford was a carpenter.

At age 30, Martha Stewart was a stockbroker.

At age 37, Ang Lee was a stay-at-home-dad working odd jobs.

At age 39, Julia Child released her first cookbook, and got her own cooking show at age 51.

At age 40, Vera Wang designed her first dress, after failing to make the Olympic figure skating team, and being passed over for Editor-in-Chief at *Vogue*.

At age 40, Stan Lee released his first big comic book.

At age 42, Alan Rickman gave up his graphic design career to pursue acting.

At age 46, Samuel L. Jackson got his first movie role.

At age 52, Morgan Freeman landed his first major movie role.

Kathryn Bigelow only reached international success when she made *The Hurt Locker* at age 57.

Grandma Moses didn't begin her painting career until age 76.

Louise Bourgeois didn't become a famous artist until she was 78.

The point here is that there is never a right time or place to be the person you want to be. If you wish to do something different, you can. Whether you go to college now, later, or never. If you adopt the mindset of a lifelong learner, and embrace an attitude of growth, you can do unimaginable things.

Conclusion

In writing this book with Elizabeth, I've had the opportunity to reflect on and be grateful for my own formal education. I graduated from Principia College in Elsah, IL with very little debt because I worked all through school. My tuition was paid for with numerous scholarships and money I'd saved from my childhood of milking cows, and selling the milk and the offspring of my cows.

I'm grateful for my upbringing (don't tell my Dad I actually liked the farm) and the hard work ethic it taught me. While not every child can live on a farm, every child can find some way to produce value and get paid. This is an incredible gift and opportunity to have, and I hope this book inspires a new generation to reach for their dreams in a multitude of ways. More than that, I hope we can collectively recognize that success has infinite faces.

Whatever your path in life, I encourage you to adopt one lesson above all else: to humble yourself as a beginner. In order to be a true "lifelong learner," you must at some points become a beginner all over again. There will be new technology, new methods, and new interests that you discover over the course of your life. You can either accept that there is a learning curve and remain curious, or you get left behind.

Thankfully, I've had a wonderful support system to help me unearth and put words to this "lifelong learning" message. Through my sister Tammi and her Blueprint Process, I now understand that my love for lifelong learning goes beyond that. If you are always learning, you're always growing. And hopefully, if you're always growing, you're always channeling that growth into serving the world and your community—whatever that looks like for you. I believe that this is the recipe for an amazing human being. If my own work can do one thing, it is to activate lifelong service in order to prevent millions of wasted lives.

— *Kim Butler*

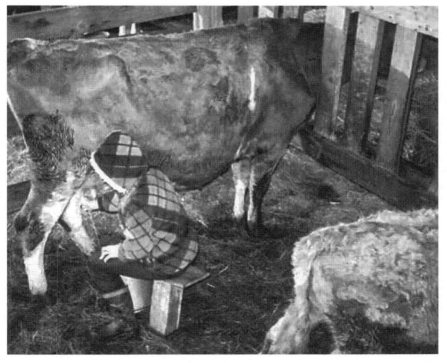

Writing this book with Kim was an interesting challenge for me, and one I'm grateful to have experienced. For me, college was a given. I never doubted that it was the right step for me to take after high school. I always loved school, and curiosity is my perpetual state of being.

That being said, funding college wasn't easy. I had the privilege of a family who wanted to help fund my education, which started with a 529 plan from my grandparents. Unfortunately, much of that account was wiped out in the 2008 recession. By the time I actually got to college, I knew I was in for some pretty significant debt. I had support along the way, but I knew I wanted to be responsible for my own education costs.

Post-college, I don't regret my decision. College helped me to become a better thinker, writer, and artist. I met some of the best friends I have. I traveled and had experiences I'll hold close to my heart forever. I do, however, wish I had been better prepared for the "what next" of paying student loans and navigating adult life. I might have made some different financial choices along the way.

While I can confidently say that the path I walked, despite the challenges, was right for me, I know others who have regrets. Ultimately, I want this book to be a guide for the kids who don't yet know what they want, so they can find more clarity. For parents, I hope this offers practical solutions to support, guide, and ultimately champion the path your child chooses for their future. Success has many faces and many paths.

— *E.P. Hagenlocher*

A Special Acknowledgment

The authors are very grateful to Mimi Klosterman and her family, who are well versed in the many unique and practical ways to obtain and finance an education. Special thanks to Annabelle and Zeke Klosterman, who provided us with their experiences around the CLEP exams and dual-credit possibilities.

Resources

Books
The Education of Millionaires by Michael Ellsberg
Tools of Titans by Tim Ferriss
Your Personality Isn't Permanent by Benjamin Hardy
The Five Love Languages by Gary Chapman
The Gap and the Gain by Dan Sullivan
Mindset: The New Psychology of Success by Carol Dweck

Personal & Professional Development Websites
Kolbe.com
BlueprintProcess.com
StrengthsFinder.com
Udemy.com
Udacity.com
Coursera.com
Unique EDGE by Strategic Coach

Financial Education Websites
TruthConcepts.com
ProsperityEconomics.org
ProsperityThinkers.com
TuttleTwins.com

Networking, Volunteering, and Freelancing
NetworkForGood.org
VolunteerMatch.org
Fiverr.com
Upwork.com
Freelance.com
LinkedIn.com
Apprenticeship.gov

Bibliography

"80 Jobs That Pay over $50k and Don't Require a Degree." U.S. Career Institute, January 20, 2021. https://www.uscareer-institute.edu/blog/80-Jobs-that-pay-over-50k-without-a-degree.

Carneval, Anthony, Neil Ridley, and Jeff Strohl. "Good Jobs That Pay without a BA." Digital Georgetown, January 5, 2018. https://repository.library.georgetown.edu/handle/10822/1047862.

Hanson, Melanie. "Average Cost of College over Time: Yearly Tuition since 1970." Education Data Initiative, January 9, 2022. https://educationdata.org/average-cost-of-college-by-year.

"History of U.S. Higher Education: Education Advisor." World Wide Learn, July 1, 2021. https://www.worldwidelearn.com/articles/history-higher-education/.

Kantrowitz, Mark. "Shocking Statistics about College Graduation Rates." Forbes. Forbes Magazine, April 21, 2022. https://www.forbes.com/sites/markkantrowitz/2021/11/18/shocking-statistics-about-college-graduation-rates/?sh=132e826d2b69loans.

"Skilled Trades: Job Satisfaction High But Labor Shortage Worsening." Staffing Industry Analysts. Accessed 2022. https://www2.staffingindustry.com/Editorial/Daily-News/Skilled-trades-Job-satisfaction-high-but-labor-shortage-worsening-59116.

USA Student Debt Relief. "The Average Cost of College in 2020." USA Student Debt Relief, November 4, 2021. https://bit.ly/3R35LeP.

About the Authors

 **Kim D. H. Butler** is helping Americans build wealth... first in their minds, with specific thinking methods, secondly on their balance sheets with life insurance cash value that grows with guarantees and finally with an income for life product that enables more guarantees and prosperous mindsets. Kim is President of Prosperity Thinkers, a money methods firm that serves clients in all 50 states. Along with her husband Todd Langford of Truth Concepts financial software, Kim is also the co-founder of the Prosperity Economics Movement.

A recognized expert on whole life insurance and financial strategies. Kim has authored paradigm-shifting books such as: *Live Your Life Insurance, Busting the Life Insurance Lies,* and *Perpetual Wealth.* She has been handling money since 4th grade when her parents gave her a milk cow. After college, she joined a bank and then a life insurance agency combined with a money management company.

Driven to find a better way, Kim studied the commonalities between wealth builders. She observed what worked and didn't work in the real world, and found synergy between certain strategies and principles. These common principles later became the 7 Principles of Prosperity so widely used.

In 1999, Kim dedicated herself to these principles of Prosperity Economics. Her work has been recommended by financial thought leaders and authors such as Robert Kiyosaki (*Rich Dad, Poor Dad*), Tom Dyson, publisher of the *Palm Beach Letter* investment newsletter, Tom Wheelright (*Tax-Free Wealth*), and Garrett Gunderson

(*Killing Sacred Cows*). She enjoys writing books (as long as she has help!) and podcasting at The Prosperity Podcast on iTunes.

You can reach Kim through ProsperityThinkers.com.

E.P. Hagenlocher is a writer and personal finance enthusiast from southern Illinois. After graduating college, she was led to work with Kim Butler on some writing projects, and the rest is history. Now she enjoys writing about financial concepts that can help people transform their lives for the better. Through this work, she hopes to make financial principles easy to understand and implement, so that financial freedom feels accessible to anyone.

About the Prosperity Economics Movement

Before the rise of qualified retirement plans, the ever-present 401(k), and the financial planning industry, people built wealth with diligence and common-sense strategies. Investors created wealth through building equity and ownership in properties, businesses, and participating (dividend-paying) whole life insurance. Only a few dabbled in Wall Street stocks or built "portfolios" on paper.

Wealthy people, in fact, have never stopped practicing what we call "Prosperity Economics."

Today, the common investor is steered away from traditional wealth-building methods. Instead, they are confronted with a confusing labyrinth of funds, rates, and complex financial instruments of questionable value. Mutual funds have become so complicated that even the people who sell them can't often explain them well, nor predict when investors are about to lose money. Worse yet, over time, over 30 percent of the average investor's wealth is drained away in fees to a financial industry rife with conflicts of interest.

The Prosperity Economics Movement (PEM) is a rediscovery of the traditional, simple, and trusted ways to grow and protect your money. It was founded in order to provide American investors an alternative to "typical" financial planning, showing us how to control our own wealth instead of delegating our financial futures to corporations and the government.

In Prosperity Economics, wealth isn't measured by how much money you have, but by how much freedom you have with your money. The focus is on cash flow rather than net worth. Liquidity, control, and safety are valued over uncertain hopes of a high rate of return.

Typical financial planning is better than nothing and will get you partway up the hill. Yet we want to show you an even better way: the top of the Prosperity mountain. Prosperity Economics shows you how to grow your wealth safely and reliably, with optimal financial flexibility and cash flow.

While Prosperity Economics Strategies and thinking have been around for many years, they were only recently coined under that term and organized as a movement by financial author Kim Butler and financial software developer Todd Langford.

The Prosperity Economics Movement is a not-for-profit organization comprising financial experts who practice Prosperity Economics and individuals who would like to learn how to apply the principles of Prosperity Economics to improve their lives. This book is part of a growing body of information that supports the organization and its members.

To learn more, visit ProsperityEconomics.org.